Your Amazing
S-Corp Book

15 Simple Steps to Understanding Everything About S-Corps

Over 25,000,000 small business owners in the USA are being unfairly targeted and overtaxed by the IRS directly contributing to millions of business failures every year. If you file your tax return as a sole proprietor, you could be one of those people. The information in this Itty-Bitty® Book will reveal the amazing benefits of turning your side hustle or small business into an S-Corporation.

Joe DiChiara, CPA will provide you with the information to learn:

- The real dangers of being taxed as a sole proprietor.

- The enormous benefits of owning an S-Corp.

- What happens after you become an S-Corp.

If you are interested in learning more about how to safely run your business and make, and hold on to, more money pickup a copy of this enlightening Itty Bitty® book today!

Your Amazing Itty Bitty® S-Corp Book

15 Simple Steps to Understanding Everything About S-Corps

Joe DiChiara, CPA

Published by Itty Bitty® Publishing
A subsidiary of S & P Productions, Inc.

Copyright © 2020 Joe DiChiara

All rights reserved. No part of this book may be reproduced or transmitted in any form or by any means, electronic or mechanical, including photocopying, recording or by any information storage and retrieval system, without written permission of the publisher, except for inclusion of brief quotations in a review.

Printed in the United States of America

Itty Bitty Publishing
311 Main Street, Suite D
El Segundo, CA 90245
(310) 640-8885

ISBN: 978-1-950326-62-4

*This book is dedicated to Nora Quinn DiChiara
my Precious Little Granddaughter.*

Stop by our Itty Bitty® website Directory to find more interesting information about corporations.

www.IttyBittyPublishing.com

Or visit our Joe DiChiara at:

bedrockbusinessbuilders.com

Table of Contents

Introduction
- Step 1. What an S-Corporation is
- Step 2. Who Should Own an S-Corporation
- Step 3. The Benefits of S-Corp Ownership
- Step 4. Legal Business Structure Alternatives
- Step 5. How to Incorporate
- Step 6. Corporate Governance
- Step 7. Corporate Name Search
- Step 8. Where to Incorporate
- Step 9. Getting IRS Approval
- Step 10. LLC vs S-Corporation
- Step 11. Late S-Corp Election Relief
- Step 12. Doing Business as an S-Corporation
- Step 13. State and Local Considerations
- Step 14. Tax Planning and Preparation
- Step 15. The Future of S-Corporations

Introduction

This book is intended for the 25,000,000 plus sole proprietors and Limited Liability Companies (LLCs) that are being unfairly targeted, overtaxed and over-audited by the IRS directly contributing to millions of business failures every year. It's also for wage earners and retirees who are tired of paying high taxes and have few options when it comes to tax and financial planning. Finally, it's for all of the future business owners who could get caught off-guard and unaware of the dangers of being taxed as a sole proprietor. Reading this book will provide you with answers to the following:

- The real dangers of being taxed as a sole proprietor.
- The enormous benefits of owning an S-Corp.
- S-Corp alternatives.
- How to create an S-Corp.
- What happens after you create an S-Corp.
- Tax planning and preparation issues.

Step 1
What An S-Corporation Is

S-Corporations were created in 1958 in response to the unfair disparity between sole proprietorships and regular corporations; the only two choices for a new business owner. Setting up a corporation was complex and expensive and so most small business owners opted not to incorporate. S-Corporation status made it less expensive by eliminating the corporate level tax while providing its shareholders with the legal protection corporations enjoy.

1. There is no federal tax on S-Corporation profits.
2. S-Corporations provide its owners with substantial tax and legal benefits compared with a sole proprietorship.
3. Doing business as an S-Corporation is the preferred way of operating a small business.
4. S-Corporations were created to give small business owners a better chance at succeeding.

Why S-Corporations are Important

S-Corporations were created to level the playing field for small business owners. With over 25,000,000 Sole Proprietors vs. only 3,000,000 S-Corporations it's obvious that this objective was never realized.

- Every business owner should know what an S-Corp is and what the tax benefits are.
- The government has failed at educating the public on S-Corporation ownership.
- S-Corporations are under-utilized.
- Doing business as an S-Corporation increases an entrepreneur's chances of success.

Step 2
Who Should Own an S-Corporation

Anyone being taxed as a sole proprietor should consider converting to an S-Corporation. Individuals working or retired in a high tax bracket can benefit from turning a side hustle or hobby into a business and elect S-Corporation status.

1. Sole Proprietors are audited more than any other business entity while S-Corps rarely get audited.
2. Sole proprietors pay self-employment tax of almost 15% on net profits while S-Corps pay 0%.
3. Wage earners and retirees can qualify for substantial tax write-offs not available to non-business owners.
4. LLC's are considered Sole Proprietors for tax purposes.

Why Sole Proprietors Should Consider S-Corp Ownership

Considering the legal protection plus tax benefits the choice of doing business as a corporation should be the first option for a new business owner.

- S-Corps were created for the benefit of sole-proprietors.
- There are over 25,000,000 business owners classified as sole proprietors for tax purposes.
- Sole proprietors should therefore consider converting to a corporate legal structure.

Step 3
The Benefits of S-Corp Ownership

S-Corp ownership comes with numerous personal, business, tax and financial planning benefits. These include significantly lower audit risks, zero self-employment tax on net profits, protection for your family, your assets, and more.

1. S-Corps have a substantially lower risk of being audited by the IRS.
2. S-Corps are not subject to self-employment taxes on net profits.
3. Pension and financial planning options available to corporate owners far outweigh what is available for sole proprietors.

Not-So-Obvious S-Corp Benefits

There are obvious benefits and many not-so-obvious benefits to owning your own S-Corporation.

- You can create business credit separate from your personal credit.
- Gain business status as a corporate owner and from being the President of your own company.
- Substantially increase your chances of success.
- Creates more business opportunities.
- Corporations can own assets outside of personal creditors reach.

Step 4
Legal Business Structure Alternatives

There are several legal structures to choose from when operating a for-profit business. Sole-proprietor (single owner), partnership (multiple owners), LLC, Corporation or S-Corporation.

1. When a business starts the default, classification is sole proprietorship.
2. If the business starts with more than 1 owner, its default classification is a partnership.
3. An LLC or LLP (Limited Liability Partnership) provide legal protection for its members.
4. Corporations and S-Corporations provide legal protection plus tax and financial benefits to its shareholders.

Why You Should Consider S-Corp Ownership

- You can safely write off business expenses.
- Wage earners and retirees can qualify for big tax benefits.
- Protects family and assets from business lawsuits.
- S-Corp ownership protects you, your family, and assets from business lawsuits.

Step 5
How to Create a Corporation

All corporations are formed at the state level through the Office of The Secretary of State in the state where the business is physically located.

1. Each state has clear instructions on how to incorporate on their websites.
2. State and local jurisdictions may have additional filing and registration requirements beyond incorporating.
3. Once incorporated you must obtain a Federal Tax Identification number at www.irs.gov.

Types of Corporations

A corporation is automatically classified as a traditional C-Corporation upon formation. There are 2 types of corporations, a traditional "C" Corp and an "S" Corporation which requires IRS approval.

- Getting incorporated is the 1st step.
- File IRS Form 2553 Election to be Treated as an S-Corporation
- States have their own separate rules on electing to be treated as an "S" Corp at the state level.

Step 6
Corporate Governance

To get the legal and tax benefits of corporate ownership you must conduct business according to the corporate rules and regulations of the state you are incorporated in.

1. Corporations are separate legal entities. The actions taken by the corporation are decided by its board of directors.
2. A single shareholder corporation can list themselves as the only board member.
3. All board decisions must be documented according to the state's rules and regulations.
4. States may require an annual meeting of the board of directors and document its decisions.

More on Corporate Governance

All the information about corporate governance can be found on each state's Secretary of State website.

- A corporation with more than 1 shareholder should consult with an attorney about corporate governance, shareholder agreements, and other matters.
- The IRS and most government guidance tout the simplicity of running a sole proprietorship while corporate governance of a single shareholder corporation is not that much more complicated.

Step 7
Corporate Name Search

Every corporation must have a unique name in the state they are doing business in. Before incorporating you must be sure the name is not already being used by another entity.

1. Each state has a corporate name search feature on its website.
2. Corporations are designated by the terms "Incorporated", "Corporation", "Limited" or by the abbreviations "Inc.", "Corp.", or "LTD" or by the words "A Professional Corporation", the abbreviation "P.C."
3. A PC (Professional Corporation) is a special designation for individuals requiring a professional license to practice i.e. Doctors, Lawyers, CPAs, and Dentists.

More on Corporate Names

You are not limited to doing business under your corporate name. By applying for a "fictitious" or "assumed" name you can have multiple brands and names under one corporate umbrella.

- You still must adhere to the unique name rules.
- Each state has their terminology and procedures for obtaining an assumed name.

Many people delay getting incorporated because they are not certain about the name they want.

- Delaying the set up will not help and can only hurt your business in the long run.
- You can always change the name you're doing business under.

Step 8
Where to Incorporate

You are required to be registered in every state you're doing business in. Each state has its own set of "Nexus" rules to determine if you're doing business there.

1. Nexus is determined by measuring the physical presence a business has in a taxing jurisdiction.
2. If you have a home-based business, you have nexus in your home state.

Why Your Home State?

Unless you live in one of the states where it is popular to incorporate like Delaware and Nevada you still need to be registered and authorized to do business in your home state.

- Single shareholder entities should incorporate in their home state unless they plan to do business (establish nexus) in other states.
- Millions of people waste time and money incorporating in the wrong state.

Step 9
Getting IRS Approval

The next step in becoming an S-Corp is to submit Form 2553 to the IRS. Until accepted, you are still a traditional C-Corp.

1. You can submit the document by mail or by fax.
2. It's imperative that your filing is documented. I use electronic fax software and receive verification when it goes through.
3. If accepted, you will be notified by mail in 6-8 weeks. You must save this document because you cannot get a copy.
4. You can elect to be an S-Corp at any time after incorporation.
5. You can also terminate an S-Corp election and revert to C-Corp status.

After Applying For S-Corp Status

An approval or rejection letter will arrive within 6-8 weeks after submission. It is imperative that you retain a copy of the letter and store it in your permanent file.

- On occasion you may need to verify IRS acceptance.
- The IRS does not reproduce the letter.
- States may claim there was no IRS approval and revoke state classification as an S-Corp.

Step 10
LLC vs S-Corporation

LLC's are not the best choice for a single owner operating entity because this status does not provide any tax benefits.

1. LLC's are taxed as sole proprietorships.
2. LLC's were created for passive investors in industries like real estate and oil wells.
3. S-Corps provide all the same legal protection of an LLCs plus the tax benefits of corporate ownership.

LLC's Are a Misused Entity

LLC's are the most misunderstood and misused type of entity. The legal argument for choosing an LLC status is that they are easier to manage than corporations.

- The documentation required to maintain a single owner corporation is minimal.
- Unless it's for a passive activity a single owner entity, in most circumstances it should be incorporated.
- An LLC can make an election to be taxed as a corporation on Form 8832 and an S-Corp on Form 2553.

You should consult with a knowledgeable tax accountant who will determine if a C-Corp or S-Corp status is more appropriate for your situation.

Step 11
Late S-Corporation Election Relief

An S-Corp election is due 75 days after the start of a new tax year or any time before the year you want the election to take place. A new corporation has 75 days from the date of incorporation to file Form 2553.

1. This rule created problems for millions of business owners who wanted to be classified as an S-Corp.
2. The IRS has created very lenient retroactive relief for up to an additional 3 years.
3. You must meet several requirements in order to qualify for late-election relief.

Who Qualifies for Late S-Corporation Election Relief

The general requirements to qualify for late election relief includes the following:

- The entity is qualified to be an S-Corp.
- There is reasonable cause for the late filing.
- That all taxes were filed consistent with being an S-Corp.
- Less than 3 years and 75 days have passed since the effective date of the election.

Step 12
Doing Business as an S-Corporation

There are state corporate governance rules and regulations that are required to maintain status as a corporation. These include:

1. Keeping books and records of business transactions.
2. Documenting business decisions.
3. Keeping personal business separate from corporate affairs.
4. The legal ramifications of not complying with state corporate rules and regulations could result in "piercing the corporate veil". This eliminates the legal and tax benefits of corporate ownership.

The Benefits of paying Yourself

One of the main benefits of S-Corp ownership is the various ways to recoup your investment and take out profits free of social security taxes.

- Reimbursing yourself for the business use of your home.
- Distributions from profits are free from social security taxes.
- Taxable salaries can be reduced by up to 25% by contributing to a pension plan.
- Health insurance becomes 100% deductible.

Step 13
State and Local Considerations

You must check with your resident state on the rules for being treated as an S-Corp at the state level and local level.

1. Some states such as California automatically accept the IRS acceptance of S-Corporation Status.
2. Most states require an additional filing to be accepted as an S-Corporation.
3. Cities such as New York City do not recognize S-Corporations and subject businesses to their own local corporate tax rate.

More Government Roadblocks

- State personal income taxes are affected by your resident states' rules on S-Corps.
- States may require additions and subtractions from income for items such as depreciation and state and local taxes deducted on your Federal tax return.
- City residents may also have tax adjustments and or credits relating to S-Corp income or losses.

Step 14
S-Corp Tax Planning

S-Corporations are considered "Pass-Through Entities". Income or losses pass through to the individual owner(s) while the entity pays no tax. This provides shareholders a level of legal protection plus a multitude of tax planning options including:

1. Converting personal property to business use property and creating legal tax deductions.
2. Deducting home office business expenses without raising red flags because of IRS record keeping requirements.
3. Options of when and how to pay yourself and maximize your social security benefits.

Why S-Corporations Are Crucial for Sole Proprietors Success

New businesses start out at a disadvantage because they are automatically considered "Sole-Proprietorships". The tax and personal liability laws put them at risk, they are overtaxed and unfairly targeted by the IRS.

- Sole Proprietorships have very few tax planning options.
- Sole Proprietors are audited significantly more than S-Corps.
- S-Corp ownership provides protections, tax savings and peace of mind.

Step 15
The Future of S-Corporations

S-Corps as we know them today may not be around much longer. This is because:

1. Many of the benefits available to S-Corp owners today may be drastically changed or eliminated.
2. Congress has been talking about making profits from S-Corps subject to social security taxes for years. This issue alone is enough to make them vulnerable.
3. The goal of helping small business owners (sole proprietors) bridge the gap between themselves and corporations never materialized.

What You Should Do Now

If you are reading this, and S-Corps are still intact I urge you to consider it your go-to legal business structure of choice.

- Join www.bedrockuniversity.com for more great business information.
- Book a Free fifteen (15) minute session with me to discuss forming your own S-Corp at www.timewithjoe.com.

You've finished. Before you go…

Tweet/share that you finished this book.

Please star rate this book.

Reviews are solid gold to writers. Please take a few minutes to give us some itty bitty feedback.

ABOUT THE AUTHOR

Mr. Joe DiChiara has worked with thousands of small business owners over a 35-year career as a Certified Public Accountant and small business advisor. Unfortunately, he watched a vast majority of these entities struggle with many barely surviving and a lot losing everything. Joe believes that much of the pain and suffering small business owners and their families experience is avoidable.

Joe's first business was driving an ice cream truck the semester before graduating with his accounting degree. This was his first real entrepreneurial endeavor! He kept "books and records", planned out his route, and expanded into wholesale…It seemed easy and Joe believed it would always be easy. He was on his way to massive success!!!

Six months into his accounting career he felt like his whole world was collapsing. Joe received a notice from The NYS Department of Finance with a big red stamp that said TAX WARRANT. What had he done? How would he ever become a CPA with this on his record? Luckily Joe was surrounded by CPA's and it turned out to be a simple fix, but that feeling of helplessness he experienced spurred him to spend many years trying to help his clients avoid that type of needless pain and suffering by providing hands-on guidance and support.

Now, Joe is going above and beyond helping his clients with Bedrock University, www.bedrockuniversity.com, Bedrock Business Building Success Blueprints and other exciting low and no-cost tools and information to help new business owners Start, Build and Manage their own small business successfully.

If you liked this Itty Bitty® Book
you might also enjoy:

- **Your Amazing Itty Bitty® Bookkeeping Book** – Joe DiChiara

- **Your Amazing Itty Bitty® Tax Audit Prevention Book** – Nellie T. Williams

- **Your Amazing Itty Bitty® Business Tax Book** – Deborah A. Morgan

Or many of the other many Itty Bitty® books available on line at ittybittypublishing.com.

Made in the USA
Las Vegas, NV
04 April 2024